D0181154

So You Think You Know About...

VELOCIRAPTOR?

BEN GARROD

So You Think You Know About...
VELOCIRAPTOR?

Kane Miller
A DIVISION OF EDC PUBLISHING

First American Edition 2019
Kane Miller, A Division of EDC Publishing

First published in the UK in 2018 by Zephyr, an imprint of Head of Zeus, Ltd
Text © Ben Garrod, 2018
Paleo Art © Scott Hartman, 2018, and Gabriel Ugueto, 2018
Cartoon illustrations © Ethan Kocak, 2018
Designed by Sue Michniewicz

The moral right of Ben Garrod to be identified as the author and of
Scott Hartman, Gabriel Ugueto and Ethan Kocak to be identified as
the artists of this work have been asserted.

All rights reserved. No part of this publication may be reproduced, stored in a
retrieval system, or transmitted in any form or by any means, electronic, mechanical,
photocopying, recording, or otherwise, without the prior permission of the publisher.

For information contact:
Kane Miller, A Division of EDC Publishing
PO Box 470663
Tulsa, OK 74147-0663
www.kanemiller.com
www.usbornebooksandmore.com
www.edcpub.com

Library of Congress Control Number: 2018958282

Printed and bound in the United States of America
1 2 3 4 5 6 7 8 9 10
ISBN: 978-1-61067-859-9

For geeky scientists
who are superheroes too

CONTENTS

I was born loving animals. I used to watch birds and squirrels and frogs in our garden and on the cliffs above the sea. When I was ten years old, I decided I would go to Africa, live with wild animals and write books about them. Everyone laughed – Africa was far away – and I was just a girl. Back then (1944), girls didn't get to do things like that. But my mother said, "If you really want this you must work hard, take advantage of opportunities, and *never give up.*" That is the message I have for you.

My dream came true when I met Dr. Louis Leakey and was able to study chimpanzees in Gombe National Park, Tanzania. Chimpanzees helped me prove to science that like humans, animals have personalities, minds and emotions. Eventually I built a research station and my students are *still* learning new things about the Gombe chimpanzees. Just as scientists are always learning about new species of dinosaur.

8

INTRODUCTION

by Jane Goodall, PhD, DBE
Founder - the Jane Goodall Institute
& UN Messenger of Peace

I have known Dr. Ben for years and he and I both encourage you to follow *your* dreams. Maybe you don't plan to be a scientist, but even so you need to learn about the work scientists do, for it helps us understand so much about the wonderful world we live in – about evolution and the incredible variety of species. And there are many more species not yet discovered. Maybe you will discover one of them! Maybe it will be named after you!

Whatever you decide to do, I hope you'll always be curious about our magical world and inspired by the people who spend their lives uncovering her secrets and sharing them. And, above all, that you will join Dr. Ben and me in our efforts to conserve life on planet Earth.

Hey, Guys

There's something you need to think about getting. You can't buy it and not everyone has it (and that's OK too), but I'd like you to try to get some. What am I talking about? **Confidence**.

It's easy to think that adults are a confident bunch and people like scientists definitely have lots of confidence but, believe me, not all are as confident as you think. So it's something I'd like you to **start practicing now**. Because if you're confident, it'll help you become a scientist more easily and might even make you a bit **better at being a scientist**.

I want you to practice in three areas for me. First, be confident in your dreams – and I don't mean the ones when you go to sleep at night. I mean the ones you have about what you want to do in life. You can do *anything*. If you want to work with space or monkeys (or even space monkeys), then please have the confidence that you *can* do it. It really doesn't matter who you are or where you're from, just remember this: you . . . can . . . do . . . anything.

All you need is passion and confidence and you've started your journey. If someone says you can't explore the deep oceans or operate on a heart or find a new species of dinosaur, have the confidence to say, "Yes I can. **I can do anything**."

The next piece of confidence advice I want you to work on is to **ask questions** and talk to people. If you're at a museum or a talk or even in class and you meet a scientist, museum curator or your number-one superstar science hero, have the confidence to say "hi" and feel free to ask a question if you have one. Remember, all these experts were young themselves once and they can remember how scary it can be to ask a question. Go for it, try it! Talk to them and see what happens.

And third, I want you to **have the confidence to be wrong**. Sounds weird, right? We always try so hard to be right. But being a good scientist means you need to be OK with being wrong a lot. And that's fine. There's nothing worse than being too scared to ask a question "in case you're wrong." Nobody should laugh at

you or be mean . . . and anyone who does is horrible. If you're wrong, so what . . . laugh it off and carry on. It **helps you learn** and be a better scientist.

I know it's not always easy to be confident but trust me, start practicing now. It's much harder to do when you're an adult.

I've had some amazing jobs – living in jungles, exploring volcanoes and sailing through Arctic storms. If I'm being honest, I've probably gotten half of my jobs partly because of my confidence. You never know where it may lead.

I've written *So You Think You Know About . . . Dinosaurs?* for a few reasons. First, I love dinosaurs and I know you do too. I wanted to write a series of science books for any young scientists out there, without dumbing them down. I have seen again and again that you guys *do* know stuff and that you hate it when adults patronize you.

Some of the stuff in these books is complicated but science isn't easy anyway. I've made them fun in a way that's straightforward to understand, and **they're packed full of new science, cool interviews with experts and fascinating facts that you won't find anywhere else.**

Let's get geeky!

Ben

CHAPTER 1

Dinosaur Definitions

WHAT *IS* A DINOSAUR?

Understanding what actually makes a dinosaur is very important to paleontologists but that's jumping ahead . . . like trying to run a race before you've even learned to walk. You need to have the basics down first. Let's look at a living animal before we look at dinosaurs, to help explain how we classify animals and plants. This process is called taxonomy (*tax-on oh-mee*).

Imagine your teacher asking you to describe what makes a chimpanzee different from other animals. You can start by separating chimpanzees from things like plants and fungi and bacteria. This level seems obvious but it's important, otherwise nothing else makes sense. This level is called the KINGDOM and chimpanzees belong to the "Animal" kingdom. Everything else starts at this level – it's the first step for looking at every species of every living (and extinct) thing. There are at least one million species in this group.

Animal

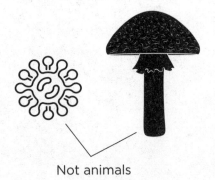

Not animals

Then we need to discover what sort of animal a chimpanzee is. The next level of group is called the PHYLUM (*fi-lum*). There are 34 different animal phylum groups, so which does the chimpanzee belong to? There are groups like the worms, the starfish and sea urchins, and insects, spiders and scorpions. Chimpanzees belong to a group called "Chordata" (*cor dat-ah*). All these animals have a spinal cord (or a simple version of one) and there are about 100,000 members of this group alive today.

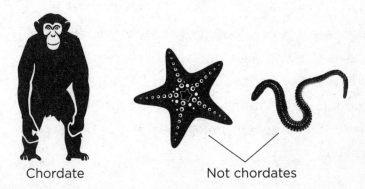

Chordate   Not chordates

Already, we've narrowed the search down from one million to 100,000. We're getting there. Let's make the search easier. There are lots of animal groups in this category – things like reptiles, amphibians and birds. These are all different types of animal CLASS. Chimpanzees belong with other similar animals that have hair and feed their young with milk – animals like dogs, cats, pigs, monkeys and elephants, mice and donkeys. This class is called "Mammalia" (*mam-male ee-ah)* and the animals are all mammals. There are about 5,500 living members in this group.

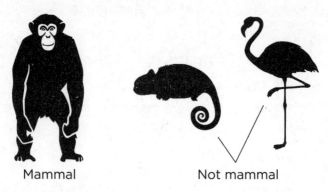

Mammal   Not mammal

There are lots of different mammals, from huge whales to flying bats, but we can separate this big group further into groups called ORDERS. You will recognize a lot of these orders. Rodents, bats, and whales and dolphins are all examples of different groups.

Chimpanzees belong to an order called the "Primates," along with other apes, monkeys and lemurs. We're not totally sure, but scientists think there are about 500 members of this group. This is a lot better than 5,000 options, a lot, lot better than 100,000 options and a lot, lot, lot better than one million options.

Primate   Not primate

Now that we know the chimpanzee is a primate, we can see if we can make the group any smaller. The next level of group is called the FAMILY. There are lots of different primate families, including lemurs, monkeys and small apes, but chimpanzees are in a group called the "Hominidae" (*hom-in-ee day*). This group is also known as the "great apes" and has only four different members.

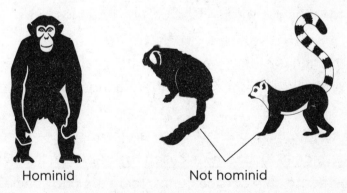

Hominid   Not hominid

We're nearly there now. The family Hominidae is made up of four different types of animal – humans, gorillas, orangutans and chimpanzees. Each of these is at the next level of classification – a level called the GENUS (*jeen-us*). Each genus has a proper name, so orangutan is "*Pongo*" and human is "*Homo*" for example. The genus name for chimpanzees is "*Pan*."

Pan   *Not Pan*

There are two little rules for describing every **genus**:

1. The genus must <u>always</u> be shown in italics – for example, *Tyrannosaurus,* not Tyrannosaurus.

2 The genus must <u>always</u> start with a capital letter – for example, *Tyrannosaurus,* not *tyrannosaurus*.

Finally, we have one last stage after the genus. This last stage in taxonomy is called the SPECIES. If we look at the chimpanzee genus, there are two species in one genus. The common names of these species are the bonobo (*paniscus*) and the actual chimpanzee (*troglodytes*).

20

troglodytes

Not *troglodytes*

There are two little rules for every **species**:

1. The species name must <u>always</u> be in italics –
for example, *rex* not rex.

2. The species must <u>always</u> start with a lowercase
(small) letter, *rex* not *Rex*.

We always write the genus and species names together.
So the chimpanzee's proper scientific name is *Pan
troglodytes*. No other living thing has this name. *THIS*
is the proper scientific name for the animal we all know
as a chimpanzee. And this system is the same for every
single dinosaur – just think of *Tyrannosaurus rex*.

We use this type of classification to understand
relationships between species, between families and
between one phylum and another. It also helps us avoid
mistakes with names. Every species has what we call a
common name and a scientific name.

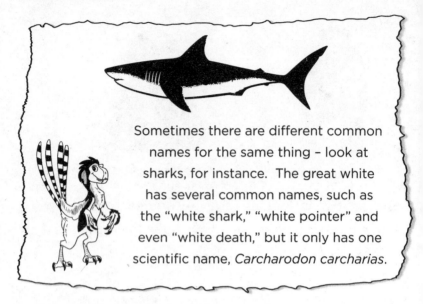

Sometimes there are different common names for the same thing – look at sharks, for instance. The great white has several common names, such as the "white shark," "white pointer" and even "white death," but it only has one scientific name, *Carcharodon carcharias*.

Here is the list of groups. As you move down the list, there are fewer and fewer members in each group. It's like a triangle turned upside down, with only one thing (the species) at the bottom.

Kingdom

Phylum

Class

Order

It can be hard to remember the order but lots of biologists use the first letter of each group to make up a memorable sentence.

Family

Genus

Species

I use this one: _**K**_ing _**P**_enguins _**C**_ome _**O**_ut _**F**_or _**G**_ood _**S**_ushi. If this one doesn't work for you, see if you can make up your own to help you remember the groups in order.

Every species has a two-part name – the genus *and* the species name. With many groups of animals, we use their common name (like "killer whale") and not their scientific name (*Orcinus orca*) but dinosaurs are different – we call *Tyrannosaurus rex* by its full scientific name. It doesn't even have a common name.

For other dinosaurs, most of us just use their genus name. For example, even though there are two *Triceratops* species (*Triceratops prorsus* and *Triceratops horridus*), we say *Triceratops*. It's the same for other dinosaurs such as *Diplodocus*, *Stegosaurus* and *Velociraptor*. Next time you read about a dinosaur, try to find out what the full name is and how many species there are.

A scientific name can often tell us something about the animal – *Hippopotamus* means "river horse" and *Homo sapiens* (for human beings) means "thinking man." Sometimes though, the name is a bit silly. The scientific name for the biggest animal ever, the blue whale is *Balaenoptera musculus*, which means "winged-whale mouse" . . . the "mouse" part was probably a joke. Ha ha!

There are some jokey or weird dinosaur names too. There's *Bambiraptor* (named after the baby deer in the Disney cartoon), *Drinker* (named after a famous paleontologist) and *Dracorex hogwartsia* (which means "Dragon King of Hogwarts").

DEFINITELY DINOSAURS

With that many species and so many looking very different, we have to be careful about deciding if a fossil is a dinosaur or not. We base the decision on just a few features of a fossil. Here are three things all dinosaurs have in common:

1. **Dinosaurs have two holes behind each eye toward the back of the skull.** This means they are diapsids.

If you're wondering, we (as mammals) belong to the synapsid group, all of which have only one hole behind each eye. When you're in your local museum, look at any dinosaur skeleton. The skull should have two holes just behind the eye.

2. **Dinosaurs all had straight legs.** Next time you see a crocodile when you're out for a walk, have a look at its legs (just don't get too close). Rather than legs that stand straight like ours, their legs bend out in

CROCODILE   DINOSAUR

the middle somewhere. All reptiles with legs, such as crocs and their relatives and many lizards, have legs that

25

look the same. They come out from the body to the side and then go down.

All dinosaurs (whether with four legs or two) walked with their legs held in a straight line beneath their body. This meant dinosaurs could breathe easily as they walked or ran – great for chasing other dinosaurs, or running away from them. It also allowed them to become much bigger than if they had legs with a bend in the middle.

3. Dinosaurs had short arms. We all know that *Tyrannosaurus rex* and its relatives had teeny arms, but almost every dinosaur had forelimbs slightly shorter than you might expect. Have a look at your arms – the upper arm bone (humerus) is only a little longer than the two lower arm bones (radius and ulna). In dinosaurs, the radius is nearly always at least 20 percent shorter than the humerus.

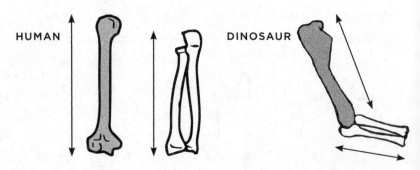

HUMAN   DINOSAUR

DINO CHECKLIST

Between the two holes behind the eye, there is a dimple (called a **fossa**) in the bone.

Most of the neck bones (**vertebrae**) have extra bits of bone that look like a little diagonally backward-facing wing on each side. These are called "**epipophyses**" (*eppi-pofe ee-sees*).

There is a ridge along the edge of the **humerus** for big muscles to attach to. In dinosaurs, this ridge is more than 30 percent of the way along the bone.

The ridge (called the **fourth trochanter**) on the **femur** (thigh bone), which the leg muscles attach to, is strong and looks "sharp."

The bones at the back of the **skull** do not meet in the middle.

The ridge on the **tibia** (shin bone) curves to the front and outward.

At the place where the **fibula** (one of the lower leg bones) joins the ankle, there's a dip on the ankle bone.

The *Velociraptor* is one of the most bird-like dinosaurs discovered so far. The arrangement of the bones of the wrist allowed them to move sideways, giving  them a flapping motion, a bit like a bird's wing. Although velociraptors definitely didn't fly, they used this ability to slash their deadly claws.

CHAPTER 2

Dinosaur Detectives

Velociraptor

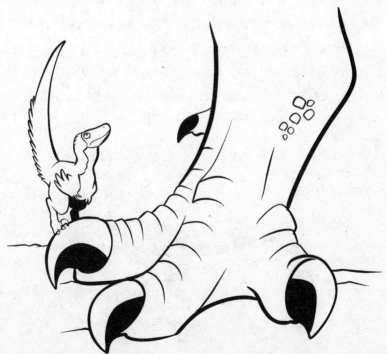

The terrifying, huge, deadly *Velociraptor* is a dinosaur we all know from books and some very famous films . . . but it is a dinosaur with a bit of an identity crisis. What most of us think about it and what science tells us is very different. Try asking adults what a *Velociraptor* looked like. I bet they say it was as tall as a human adult, scaly like a lizard, with big scary teeth and even bigger scary claws used to rip the guts out of its prey. If they do say this they're entirely wrong.

Velociraptor's claws were its greatest weapon, but they weren't used to rip out the guts of its victims, and it did have sharp serrated teeth, but they weren't very big. It was not scaly but covered in feathers, and the biggest surprise of all is that it was not a huge killer but about the size of a turkey. A deadly dinosaur but not in the way it is in the movies.

Velociraptor was a small, two-legged predatory dinosaur. It was about the height of a big turkey but about 6 ft. long. The name *Velociraptor* means "*fast thief*" (*veloci-* meaning "*fast*" and *raptor* meaning "*thief*" or "*taker*"). *Velociraptor* lived 75–71 million years ago in the Late Cretaceous.

Although there might be two different species of *Velociraptor* – *Velociraptor mongoliensis* and *Velociraptor osmolskae* – it is possible that one is an imposter. *Velociraptor osmolskae* might not be a velociraptor at all. It might be more closely related to another small raptor called *Tsaagan* (which scientists also thought was a *Velociraptor* when it was found). The truth is that we don't fully know yet, but more research might reveal the true identity of this *Velociraptor* wannabe.

The first *Velociraptor* fossils were found in the 1920s. Paleontologists from the American Museum of Natural History realized that Mongolia was one of the most remote and unexplored places on Earth. There were no train stations or airports and only sturdy cars or horses could get around. They thought it would be a great place to look for interesting new fossils and they were right.

The group was led by the famous fossil-hunter Roy Chapman Andrews, who found the first *Oviraptor* and *Protoceratops* fossils, but he didn't find the first *Velociraptor* fossils. One of his team found a broken-up skull and a toe claw in the desert. Even at the start, there was confusion with *Velociraptor.* It was given a different name. Originally, it was called the *Ovoraptor*. Imagine the confusion if we had *Ovoraptor* and *Oviraptor*. Luckily, *Ovoraptor* was quickly renamed and *Velociraptor* is a name we are not going to forget now.

Velociraptor had a long tail and a large special claw on each back foot. This claw was curved and very sharp and was the weapon that makes the dinosaur so famous. It belongs to a group of predators called the dromaeosaurs (known as the "raptors") and so far, more fossils have been found for *Velociraptor* than for any of the other raptor dinosaurs.

FAMILY TREE

Velociraptor was a dromaeosaur (*dro me-ay oh-sore*) dinosaur and belonged to a group called the Dromaeosauridae (*Dro me oh-sore idd-ayy*). The name dromaeosaur means "running lizards" and these were fast, two-legged carnivorous dinosaurs. Dromaeosaur fossils have been found across the world, from North America and Europe, to Mongolia, Africa and even Antarctica.

a) *Microraptor gui* b) *Dromaeosaurus albertensis* c) *Austroraptor cabazai*
d) *Velociraptor mongoliensis* e) *Utahraptor ostrommaysorum*
f) *Deinonychus antirrhopus*

What did the dromaeosaurs have in common? They were small to medium-sized two-legged carnivores and scientists think that most, if not all, were covered in feathers. And not the weird sort of little fluffy feathers that some of the big theropod dinosaurs had and birds such as kiwis have today. Many dromaeosaurs had large feathers, with a central vane (the thin, stiff strip usually somewhere near the middle, that runs from top to bottom of a feather), which may have allowed flight. Dromaeosaurs also had a fairly big skull, with a narrow snout. They had forward-facing eyes and sharp, serrated teeth.

Dromaeosauridae includes a large number of dinosaurs, split into several different groups, with some well-known animals such as *Microraptor*, *Utahraptor* and *Deinonychus*.

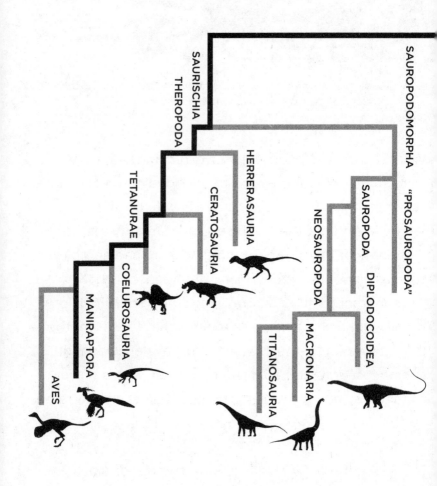

DINOSAURIA

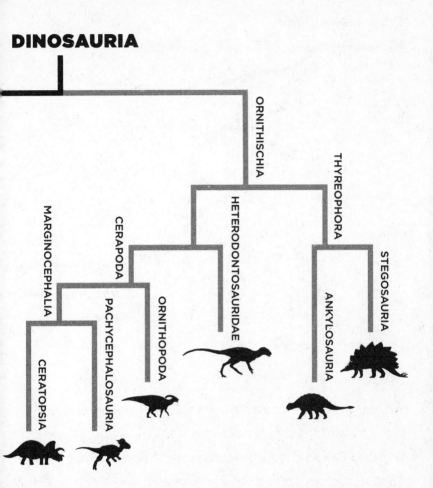

ORNITHISCHIA

THYREOPHORA

MARGINOCEPHALIA

CERAPODA

HETERODONTOSAURIDAE

STEGOSAURIA

PACHYCEPHALOSAURIA

ORNITHOPODA

ANKYLOSAURIA

CERATOPSIA

Velociraptor represents one branch in this family tree. The dromaeosaurs appeared in the Early Cretaceous (over 125 million years ago). They were around for over 50 million years, until the end of the Cretaceous, when the famous asteroid struck, 66 million years ago.

35

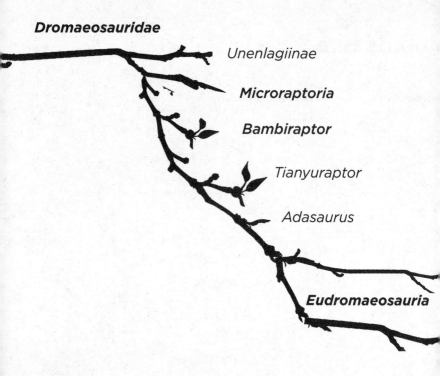

Dromaeosauridae

Unenlagiinae

Microraptoria

Bambiraptor

Tianyuraptor

Adasaurus

Eudromaeosauria

Although the *Velociraptor* branch is on its own, there were other closely related species. These species are in a group called the Dromaeosaurinae and include raptors such as *Deinonychus*, *Dromaeosaurus* and *Dakotaraptor*. All these animals had something special – they had a large, curved, sharp claw on their second toe, used for killing prey and maybe for climbing trees. Scientists think that when these dinosaurs walked, they held this claw up off the ground, so it was not damaged.

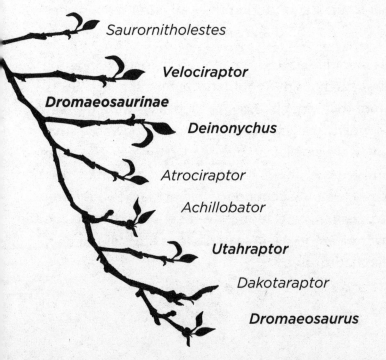

Tsaagan

Saurornitholestes

Velociraptor

Dromaeosaurinae

Deinonychus

Atrociraptor

Achillobator

Utahraptor

Dakotaraptor

Dromaeosaurus

VELOCIRAPTOR RELATIVES

Deinonychus (*Di-no ni-kus*) "terrible claw"

There was only one species of *Deinonychus.* Fossils have been found in places across the US, including Montana, Utah, Wyoming and Oklahoma. Teeth have been found farther east in Maryland. These raptors lived 115–108 million years ago (during the Early Cretaceous period) and grew to about 11 ft. in length.

This medium-sized dromaeosaur helped change the way scientists thought about dinosaurs in the late 1960s. Before that, people thought dinosaurs were big, slow and mostly useless but *Deinonychus* showed us that many were small, fast and deadly hunters. The name "terrible claw" refers to the big curved talon on the second toe of each hind foot. In at least two different sites, *Deinonychus* teeth have been found alongside the fossils of *Tenontosaurus* (a close relative of the duck-billed hadrosaurs).

Utahraptor (*U-ta rap-tor*) "Utah's robber"

There was also only one species of *Utahraptor* and it's not a huge surprise that the fossils have all been found in Utah. These raptors lived in the Early Cretaceous period, about 126 million years ago, give or take 2.5 million years either side of this date.

Utahraptor was the largest of the dromaeosaurid raptors. At up to 12 ft. and 1100 lb., it was about the same weight as a polar bear but twice the length. It had raptor claws, which could grow around 8 in. long. In one amazing fossil, the skeletons of six *Utahraptors* were found in fossilized quicksand. They had been either attacking or scavenging on an *Iguanodon* relative. In this fossil, one adult, four young animals and one baby were found, meaning they may have hunted in groups or even lived in families.

Microraptor (*My-kro rap-tor*) "little robber"

There were up to three *Microraptor* species. All lived in the Early Cretaceous period, roughly 120 million years ago, and many of their fossils have been found in China, in a place called Liaoning. This is one of the best fossil sites in the world for well-preserved feathered dinosaurs.

As the name suggests, this was a small raptor. It was rarely longer than 31 in. and weighed about 2 lb. It had four wings (attached to its legs as well as its "arms") and it could glide between trees – some scientists believe it could actually fly, as well as glide. Some of the fossils have striped feathers, meaning it may have had "striped" colors when it was alive, and research has shown it was iridescent, like starlings are today. *Microraptor* fossils are important, as they help scientists better understand the relationship between birds and dinosaurs.

Dromaeosaurus (*Dro may-o sore-us*) "fast running lizard"

There is only one species of *Dromaeosaurus*. These raptors lived during the Late Cretaceous, between 76.5 and 74.8 million years ago, and their fossils have been found in the western United States and in Alberta, Canada.

This was a medium-sized raptor, weighing about 33 lb. and measuring roughly 6 ft. long. It had a shorter skull than its relatives and its jaws were much tougher. Its teeth were also stronger and more solid than those of other raptors and it was thought to have a bite force at least three times greater than the *Velociraptor*. It appears that *Dromaeosaurus* was crushing its prey, not just tearing flesh. This is a popular dinosaur in books and films, and there are lots of museum models but there are only a few actual *Dromaeosaurus* fossils.

So You Think You Know About Dinosaurs?

Which phylum does the chimpanzee belong to?

•

What does *Homo sapiens* mean?

•

Which part of an animal's name comes first –
genus or species?

•

What group does *Velociraptor* belong to?

•

When did velociraptors first appear and how long
did they survive?

•

Name one of the best sites for
finding feathered dinosaurs.

***All the answers are in the text
and at the back of the book.***

CHAPTER 3

Dinosaur Discoveries

WHEN AND WHERE

WHEN AND WHERE

The times the dinosaurs existed can be split into three main chunks of time (what we call "periods"). These are the **Triassic period**, the **Jurassic period** and the **Cretaceous period**. All time periods fit inside a bigger chunk of time (an "era") and these three periods are inside the Mesozoic Era.

The Mesozoic Era is also called "The Time of the Dinosaurs." Velociraptors were around in the Late Cretaceous. They appeared about 76 million years ago and died out about 71 million years ago.

All known *Velociraptor* fossils have come from the Gobi Desert, an area that covers southern Mongolia and northern China. If you want to be really specific, then *Velociraptor mongoliensis* fossils have been found in a place called the Djadochta Formation, which is famous for the Flaming Cliffs.

This beautiful area is made from red and orange sandstone and it is famous for the large number of fossils that have been found there. Dinosaur eggs were

The Flaming Cliffs

THE WORLD IN THE LATE CRETACEOUS PERIOD

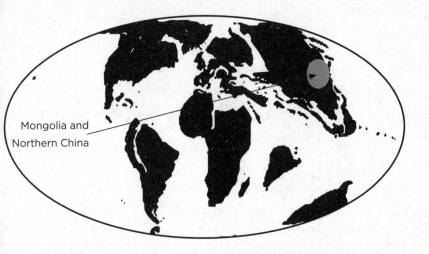

Mongolia and
Northern China

first discovered in this region and lots of *Velociraptor* and early mammal fossils are still being found there today.

Fossils from the other species (*Velociraptor osmolskae*) have so far only been discovered in a place known as the Bayan Mandahu Formation which is in Southern Mongolia.

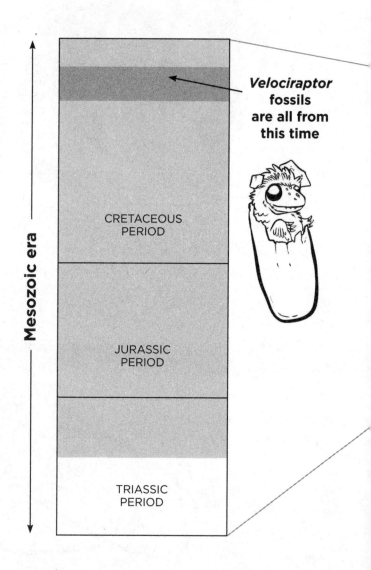

Velociraptor fossils are all from this time

Mesozoic era

CRETACEOUS PERIOD

JURASSIC PERIOD

TRIASSIC PERIOD

MILLIONS OF YEARS AGO	GEOLOGICAL PERIOD	GEOLOGICAL ERA TODAY
	Holocene	
First human beings	Pleistocene	Cenozoic
1.8		
	Pliocene	
	Miocene	
First cats	Oligocene	
	Eocene	
	Paleocene	
Dinosaurs extinct 66		
First bees	Cretaceous	Mesozoic
First birds	Jurassic	
First mammals		
First dinosaurs	Triassic	
225	Permian	
First reptiles	Carboniferous	Paleozoic
First amphibians	Devonian	
	Silurian	
First land plants	Ordovician	
570	Cambrian	
First fish		
1000		Proterozoic
2000		
First multicelled organisms		
3000		
First life evolves – single cell 4000		Archaean

47

In many famous films, velociraptors are nearly always shown as massive predatory raptors, bigger even than a human being. This giant raptor did exist but it wasn't *Velociraptor* — it was *Deinonychus*. *Velociraptor* was a much smaller dinosaur, about the size of a  turkey or very large chicken. The next time you see a huge *Velociraptor* in a film, make sure you shout out this case of prehistoric mistaken identity.

How do museums take care of fossils?

So many people work with dinosaurs –
from amateur collectors to world-famous scientists.
Some go looking for fossils in the ground, others study
them in laboratories and some recreate them
as incredible pieces of artwork.

ISLA GLADSTONE

Senior Curator for the Natural Sciences collections
Bristol Museum & Art Gallery (UK)

Isla Gladstone is a paleontologist who works
in a museum. She manages a team taking care of
a collection of more than a million
geology and biology specimens.

Have you ever been to a museum and seen fossils on display? Perhaps you have a favorite dinosaur skeleton you like to visit, or look at in photos. Did you know there might be hundreds, thousands or even millions more fossils stored in special vaults at the museum? Imagine rows and rows of drawers and boxes containing fossils . . . any one could reveal something brand-new about prehistoric life to a visiting paleontologist, or be part of a new event, TV show or museum display.

It is a curator's job to take care of all these fossils.

First, we need to be able to find any one fossil among all the others. Each has a unique code, usually made up of numbers and letters like "Cb8756" or "1991.1G." This code is listed in a register with a note about where the fossil is stored within the museum because sometimes, there might be several million fossils in a museum collection.

Next, we add information about the fossil such as its name, the place and layer of rock it was discovered in and who found it. The more information we record, the more useful it is to scientists. For example, if you know which layer of rock a fossil came from, you can work out its age.

To help our fossils survive into the future, we protect them in two ways. First, careful packing prevents bumps and breaks – ideally each fossil has its own tray within a bigger drawer or box. Second, an environment that is not too damp or too dry slows down chemical reactions in fossils that might otherwise turn them furry, release burning acids, or even cause them to explode!

Fossils can arrive at the museum still buried inside tons of rock. At Bristol Museum, we have a 26-ft.-long Pliosaurus fossil that took ten years to uncover! The rock it was in was carefully chipped away using a chisel, a scalpel and a special tool that blasts away tiny specks of rock with a stream of air.

To plan a new display, we have to find specimens we think will make people go "Wow!" They also need to have a good story. Piecing a big dinosaur skeleton together for display can be a tricky task. Sometimes we use digital scans of the bones to plan where each bone will go in virtual space. Illustrations, models, noises and smells help bring a display to life.

Museums have been collecting fossils for a very long time. Some fossils might have been in the museum since before the word "dinosaur" was even invented. These can still reveal brand-new things about prehistoric life as scientists discover new ways to investigate them or look at them with new knowledge.

If you have your own collection of fossils you can take care of them in the same way museums do. Remember to give each a unique code, record information about it, and keep it safe. Then create your own displays so other people can enjoy your finds.

CHAPTER 4

Delve into a Dinosaur

ANATOMY OF *VELOCIRAPTOR*

THE BONES

Many people think that predatory dinosaurs were usually big, heavy animals and that they were often covered in spikes, spines and armor. But not all were like this. Some were small, fast and deadly. If *Tyrannosaurus rex* was like a deadly monster truck then *Velociraptor* was like a race car – streamlined, light and speedy, perfect for chases and deadly strikes.

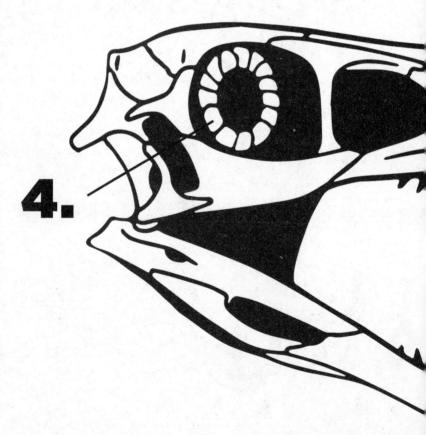

4.

THE SKULL

Velociraptor was a fast and deadly predator. It didn't have a massive skull like a *Tyrannosaurus rex* and its skeleton wasn't huge like that of *Giganotosaurus*, but it was still a killer with lots of very special bone-based adaptations.

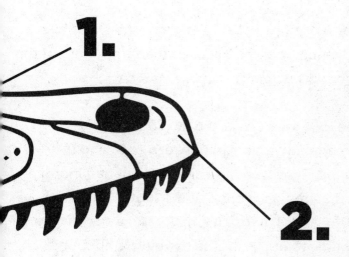

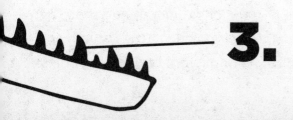

1. The skull is special because it is the only dinosaur skull that slightly curves up. On the upper surface, it is what we call concave (with a dip) and on the lower surface it is convex (with a bulge). This might sound complicated but basically, it had a shape similar to a banana (but with teeth and not yellow).

2. The skull grew up to 10 in. long. The snout was long and made up more than half the total length of the skull (about 60 percent).

3. The long jaws contained 26–28 teeth. The teeth were spread out with a gap between each and they were curved. They were also serrated but had more serrations on the back edge of the tooth. This may have allowed the animal to use its mouth like a saw, slicing off chunks of meat and flesh. The teeth were about half an inch long.

4. Velociraptors had a ring of bone in each eye socket to help give the eyeball shape and more strength. The shape and arrangement of these rings, called sclerotic rings (*s-klair rot-ik),* are different for animals that are active during the day (diurnal) and those active at night (nocturnal). After looking at their shape and comparing them to the rings from birds and reptiles alive today, scientists think that velociraptors may have been nocturnal, hunting at night when their desert habitat was cooler.

The front edges of *Velociraptor* teeth were smooth but with a sharp edge, like a small, sharp dagger.

The back edges of *Velociraptor* teeth were ridged and serrated, like a bread knife. Each little serration was sharp, making it an efficient cutting surface.

The two sides of *Velociraptor*'s teeth worked together, one side slicing through muscle and the other cutting through tougher ligaments and tendons, like a very sharp, very dangerous knife.

THE SKELETON

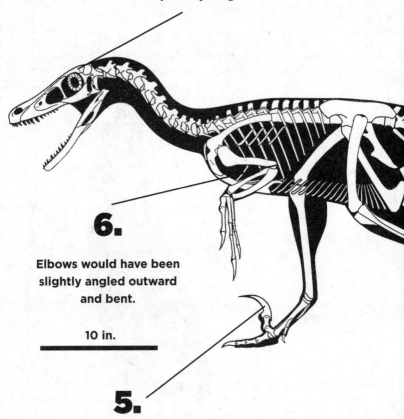

1.

Velociraptor skulls were especially long.

6.

Elbows would have been slightly angled outward and bent.

10 in.

5.

The claw on the second digit of the foot was large and held up off the ground.

2.

A *Velociraptor* tail had special extra bits of bone that were on top of the vertebrae.

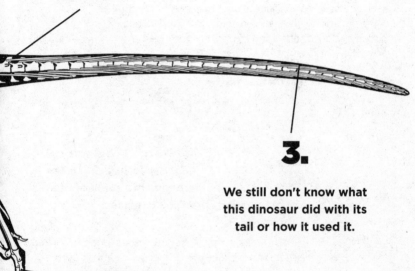

3.

We still don't know what this dinosaur did with its tail or how it used it.

4.

The *Velociraptor* walked on two digits – toes three and four.

1. *Velociraptors* had especially long skulls.

Although all the dromaeosaurid dinosaurs had long skulls, the *Velociraptor* skull was especially long and the snout pointed slightly upward at the end.

2. A *Velociraptor* tail had special extra bits of bone that were on the top of the vertebrae.

These were called prezygapophyses (*pre zy-go po-fee-seez*) and started at the tenth tail vertebrae. Each was a long, thin strip of bone that helped keep other vertebrae in place. Some ran along four other vertebrae and others ran along ten. For a long time, scientists thought that these strips made the tail solid and unable to bend . . .

3. . . . but one *Velociraptor* specimen has been found with some of the tail vertebrae still in place.

On this fossil, the tail was curved in an S-shape. This means that right now, we still don't really know what this dinosaur did with its tail or how it used it.

4. *Velociraptor* only walked on two digits.

Most theropod dinosaurs walked with three claws on the ground. There was a fourth toe but it was little and halfway up the foot. This is called the dewclaw (and lots of animals, such as dogs, still have them now). But dromaeosaurid dinosaurs like *Velociraptor* only walked on two digits, toes three and four.

5. *Velociraptor* had a retractable claw.

This might be the most famous "finger" ever. The claw on the second digit of the foot was very large, curved and held up off the ground. It was what we call retractable, just like the claw of a lion or a house cat. It was also very, very sharp! For years, scientists thought that maybe *Velociraptor* used these awesome weapons to rip open the bodies of its victims – that's definitely what we see in films, anyway.

We now think that this 2.5-in.-long killer claw couldn't be used to slice flesh. Instead, it was probably used to stab prey, delivering the death blow.

6. The *Velociraptor* hand was large with three long digits (fingers) ending in strong curved claws.

In many ways, the hand looked like the wings of birds alive today and of species like *Archaeopteryx*. The first digit was the shortest and the second digit was the longest. The bones in the hand (the carpals) fitted together in a way that meant the hands were held facing one another and not with the "palms" facing downward.

If we look at three very different animals like a *Velociraptor*, *Archaeopteryx* and a bird, we can see how a few tweaks and changes here and there can turn a hand into a wing in just a few million years. It might seem like a long time but it's the blink of an eye when you're talking about evolution.

Velociraptor   *Archaeopteryx*   Bird

THE BODY

The *Velociraptor* is in the middle of one of the biggest examples of mistaken identity anywhere in the animal kingdom. There are some famous dinosaur films out there with huuuuuge velociraptors – as tall as an adult human. Here's the surprise . . . these aren't actually *Velociraptor* at all but probably *Deinonychus*.

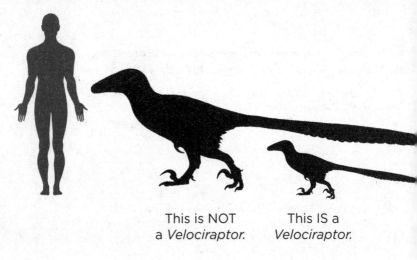

This is NOT
a *Velociraptor.*

This IS a
Velociraptor.

Our understanding of the appearance of *Velociraptor* has changed over the years. As scientists have found more fossils and have better techniques and equipment, we have a much better idea about what they looked like.

It was only in the late 1990s and early 2000s that we realized that velociraptors were probably feathered, because lots of fossils have now been found from related species and they all have feathers. The problem then was whether they were feathered all over or just on parts of the body, and what were the feathers like? Were they modern feathers like we see on most birds, or were they "fluffy" like those on kiwis and other flightless birds? And did *Velociraptor* have wings or not?

Because we know *Velociraptor* had feathers, it is extremely likely that it was warm-blooded (or endothermic). This would have meant it had a faster and more effective metabolism than other dinosaurs such as *Protoceratops*, which was probably cold-blooded (ectothermic) and relied on the outside environment to warm it up.

Being endothermic would have been really useful for predatory dinosaurs that may have hunted at night.

THE BODY

1.

We think it had "lips" that went over its teeth.

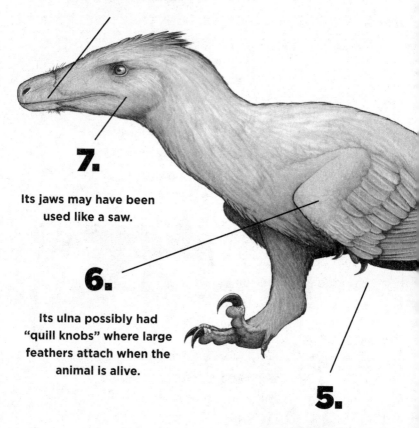

7.

Its jaws may have been used like a saw.

6.

Its ulna possibly had "quill knobs" where large feathers attach when the animal is alive.

5.

Its forelimbs would have looked more like wings with big claws at the end.

3.

Its tail looked like
a fan made from
feathers.

2.

An adult would have
weighed 28-40 lb.

4.

Maybe the *Velociraptor* used
its claw like eagles do, to
hold and pin down prey.

1. We now think that *Velociraptor* (like many of the theropods with teeth) had "lips" that went over its teeth. For a long time, dinosaurs were drawn with the teeth always showing, but scientists now believe that their mouths were more similar to reptiles such as Komodo dragons, rather than crocodiles.

2. A fully grown adult *Velociraptor* would have weighed 28-40 lb. (about as much as a baboon or a medium-sized dog).

3. Its tail looked like a fan made from feathers, which were attached to the long central tail. Because the tail was probably made fairly stiff by the thin bony strips between the vertebrae, it was possibly used for balance when the dinosaur was running, climbing or jumping on struggling prey.

4. People often think that *Velociraptor* used its claw to rip open the bodies of its victims. But scientists found that its claws look similar to those of eagles, hawks and vultures and they kill their prey by jumping onto them, holding them down and pinning them with their curved claws. In the famous fossil known as the "Fighting Dinosaurs" (read the dino battle on page 86), the prey of a *Velociraptor* had a claw stabbed in its neck. Maybe this is how *Velociraptor* killed, using its supersized claw to pierce arteries and veins in the throat.

5. Its forelimbs would have looked more like wings with big claws at the end. These wing-arms were probably held close to the body and folded up, like a bird wing.

6. In 2007, a special *Velociraptor* fossil was found. An ulna (one of the bones between the elbow and wrist) was discovered and it had little bumps on it.

These are known as "quill knobs" and are where large feathers attach when the animal is alive. Many birds that fly have them today but having them doesn't mean the animal definitely flies . . . so don't get excited, *Velociraptor* did not fly! We can be certain that it was feathered though, and that its feathers were like those of the birds we see now.

7. Its jaws were not strong but may have been used like a saw, pulling through skin and muscle. Komodo dragons use their jaws like this, helping them tear up their prey.

So You Think You Know About Dinosaurs?

Which desert have *Velociraptor* fossils been found in?

•

How many teeth did a *Velociraptor* have?

•

What did *Velociraptor* use its 2.5-in. claws for?

•

What does endothermic mean?

•

How much did a *Velociraptor* weigh?

•

How many fingers did *Velociraptor* have?

All the answers are in the text and at the back of the book.

CHAPTER 5

Dinosaur Domains

HABITATS AND ECOSYSTEMS

HABITATS AND ECOSYSTEMS

All the *Velociraptor* fossils have been found in the Gobi Desert. Today, there's not much vegetation and it's very dry and really, really hot. Back in the Cretaceous, it was pretty much the same but with a few more plants and some streams and lakes here and there.

These hot and dry conditions mean not only that fossils have been well preserved but also that when the animals were alive, life would have been tough. The habitat would have been mainly sand dunes, with only limited fresh water from streams and oases. There were also some areas of thick conifer forests.

Now, the Gobi Desert has some extreme temperature shifts, from an unbelievably hot 113°F during the summer to a bone-shattering cold -40°F in winter. The same habitat over 70 million years ago probably had the same temperatures, showing just how hard this place was to survive in.

Because the Gobi during the Cretaceous was such a tough place to live, even plants had a problem. Without much vegetation, the herbivores could not grow big, so there were only small species in the area. Because the herbivores were small, most of the carnivores were small too. Only a few of the predators in the area, like *Tarbosaurus*, were big. The rest were not even as large as an adult human. The only other big dinosaur in the area was the wonderfully weird *Therizinosaurus*.

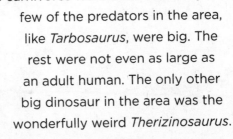

There weren't too many dinosaur species walking around the Gobi Desert at the same time as *Velociraptor,* but of the ones that were there, only a few were well known. Which ones do you recognize?

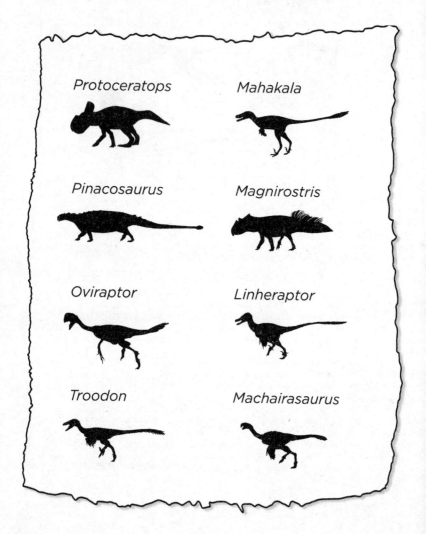

Protoceratops

Mahakala

Pinacosaurus

Magnirostris

Oviraptor

Linheraptor

Troodon

Machairasaurus

Velociraptor fossils have been found in two areas in the Gobi Desert. See if you can spot something weird about them and some other dinosaurs commonly found in the desert ecosystem:

DJADOCHTA FORMATION	BAYAN MANDAHU FORMATION
Velociraptor mongoliensis	*Velociraptor osmolskae*
Protoceratops andrewsi	*Protoceratops hellenikorhinus*
Pinacosaurus grangeri	*Pinacosaurus mephistocephalus*

The two main rock formations each have a species of *Velociraptor, Protoceratops* and *Pinacosaurus* but something has to make this possible – species don't just change like this.

Something physical like an ocean, mountains or even a big river can cut one group off from another, and over time they become different enough to be called different species. But there was nothing physical keeping these animals from each other. Instead, scientists think the two groups of dinosaurs may have lived at different times, allowing them to become separate groups.

Both *Tarbosaurus* and *Therizinosaurus* were also found in the same area but were there around 70 million years ago, so they may have overlapped with *Velociraptor.*

Evolution after the asteroid strike

Piecing together what happened in the past is not always easy . . . if we want to find out what happened yesterday, we can look on the internet. If we want to look at something from 50 years ago, there's maybe something on TV and from one hundred years ago, maybe the radio or letters. All of these ways to record history are great at giving us a lot of details but imagine if we want to know what happened 66 million years ago. There was no internet, no TV, no radio, no letters . . . instead, we have to piece together little bits of fossils. It's like listening to a story but only hearing every twentieth word.

We know what life was like just before an asteroid struck Earth around 66 million years ago, and thanks to some brand-new research, we even know a lot about what happened *when* it struck, but what happened *after*? How long did it take for all the non-avian dinosaurs (the ones that wouldn't evolve into birds) to die out? When did all the species we know today start popping up? What did these new species look like?

Well, a new fossil has just been found that helps us understand more about what happened after the asteroid struck the sea north of what is now Mexico. Bird fossils from this time are very rare indeed but this

little fossil shows that
birds (as we know them
now) started evolving very
quickly after all the other dinosaurs
died out.

Remember that evolution still takes a long time,
so even though this little fossil dates from 66 million
years ago (four million years *after* the asteroid), this is
still pretty quick in terms of evolution. It would be like
the time between getting up in the morning and having
breakfast – no time at all.

We know that groups such as mammals and birds
survived the asteroid, which killed off around 75 percent
of life on Earth. But because birds have bones that are
often tiny and usually very delicate, they are not great

at being fossilized. This one discovery in Mexico shows two things. First, within four million years, modern-looking birds had evolved and second, that different groups that we know now were there – things such as owls and other raptors, kingfishers and woodpeckers – had all appeared by then.

So, what did this fossil look like? And which bird was it? It's a little bird that many of you will never have heard of – it's quite weird and nowadays only has a limited range. It's a mousebird.

Little bones from the legs were found – they were broken up but scientists are able to predict what the rest of the bones looked like (as well as the rest of the skeleton).

Lots of little bits of fossilized bones were found. Here is a right femur (thigh bone) on the left and a left tarsometatarsus (some of the "ankle" and foot bones that have fused together in birds and some dinosaurs) on the right. The bits in black are the bits of bones the scientists found.

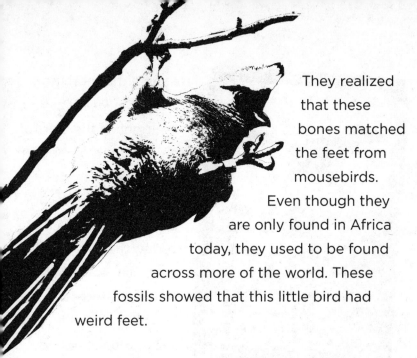

They realized that these bones matched the feet from mousebirds. Even though they are only found in Africa today, they used to be found across more of the world. These fossils showed that this little bird had weird feet.

It could do something that very few birds can do – it could rotate one of its toes to face backward (imagine being able to do that). This meant it could climb through branches and hold on better. This little fossilized bird would have lived high up in the trees – what we call a "crown bird." This very special adaptation is called zygodactyly (*zy-go dac-til-ee*) and means two toes face forward and two face backward.

A mousebird foot from below, showing zygodactyly.

Scientists called this little bird *Tsidiiyazhi abini* (*siddy ya-zee a-binn-ee*), which

VELOCIRAPTOR

SPEED	9
AVERAGE WEIGHT	1
AGILITY	8
WEAPONS (teeth, horns)	7

means "little morning bird" because it was alive right at the start of the evolution of modern birds. Although we know of around 10,000 species of birds alive today, this one fossil helps show us that birds started evolving quickly after the asteroid strike and that even very early on, some birds we would recognize today had appeared.

PROTOCERATOPS

SPEED	2
AVERAGE WEIGHT	2
AGILITY	3
WEAPONS (teeth, horns)	4

CHAPTER 6

Dodging Dinosaurs

EVOLUTIONARY ARMS RACE

EVOLUTIONARY ARMS RACE

It's always worth remembering that every species alive (or that has ever been alive) is at the mercy of its environment. Each habitat and ecosystem has a huge influence on the species living there. Great white sharks have a white belly and gray-blue body, so that prey can't see them from above or below. Peregrine falcons have lightweight bones and excellent vision for hunting high in the sky and can fly at speeds of over 185 miles per hour. As well as environments affecting species physically in terms of color and eyesight, they also affect behaviors.

In the Late Cretaceous, some parts of Earth were as hot and dry as they are today. Mongolia was one of them and the land would have been mainly desert with little patches of scrubby forest. High daytime temperatures would have forced many animals to shelter, only coming out when the sun went down. In such a harsh landscape, where there was never a guarantee of a meal, some predators may have hunted in groups to have a better chance of killing prey.

THE BATTLE

In this battle, we see a group of hunters, out at night, looking for prey. Three velociraptors are hunting, working together to flush prey from the rocks. They are not actually cooperating like lions or wolves do. Each is hunting alone but knows its chances of success are increased in a group. As one scares a small lizard or mammal from the rocks, another darts in and eats it. That way, each gets a little more food than if they hunted alone.

Lots of animals hunt together but not all are intentionally helping each other. Blacktip reef sharks swim in large groups at night over a reef. Each will swim under and beneath corals to chase out fish. They may not catch those fish but other sharks in the  group will snap them up. Even though each shark only wants to feed itself, they all have a better chance of a meal if they hunt in a gang like this.

Now, as the sun has finally set and the moon has turned the landscape silver, one *Velociraptor* spots a possible prey. Feathers around his head rustle with excitement and the others know he is on to something. *Velociraptor* fossils show us that velociraptors had large eyes with a ring of bony plates inside to give them extra support. Although we may never know for sure, this may have made these dinosaurs excellent night hunters. One predator walks to the edge of the very high sand dune and peers down, to where a *Protoceratops* is feeding on a thorny bush.

The *Protoceratops* is part of the horned dinosaur group (the ceratopsids), like *Triceratops*. But unlike her giant cousin, she is the size of a pig. She's still strong and has defensive horns and a crest. She's too big for a single *Velociraptor* but maybe three together stand a chance of taking her down. The velociraptors run down the steep sand dune toward the little herbivore. There is a strong wind blowing, so she cannot hear them approaching and her small eyes are almost useless at

night. As the velociraptors run toward their prey, they keep their heads low and their stiff tails high up in the air.

One *Velociraptor* leaps onto the back of the *Protoceratops*, taking her by surprise. She bellows and throws her head about, knocking the predator off. The *Velociraptor* leaps up again and all three surround her, mouths open wide, exposing their sharp curved teeth. The *Protoceratops* is an aggressive animal and stamps, as she tosses her head side to side to threaten the predators.

One *Velociraptor* is near the rear of the *Protoceratops*. He leaps onto her hips and sinks the large curved claw on his foot into the muscle of her thigh. The skin there is tough but she is bleeding now. The wind is stronger and louder and sand blows from the dune, stinging the velociraptors' large eyes. As the injured *Protoceratops* tries to throw off her attacker, another *Velociraptor* rushes in, trying to stab one of his deadly claws into her throat. These claws can't be used to rip open and tear flesh but they are lethal stabbing weapons. His long legs stretch forward and he grabs on to the crest of her skull as he stabs his claws deep into her shoulder.

89

She roars in pain, half throwing off the new attacker. He slips and tries to hold on to her face but the angry *Protoceratops* bites hard into his wrist and shakes him violently. He releases his sharp claw from her shoulder as her beaked jaw crushes his muscles and bones. He hisses in pain and the other two predators retreat, as the injured *Protoceratops* shakes him around, his body twisting wildly.

The *Protoceratops* falls to her knees. She's badly injured and has lost a lot of blood but she still bites hard into her attacker, breaking more bones and damaging flesh. The two other velociraptors see she will soon be an easy kill and move in once more.

The wind howls across the desert. The dune that the three velociraptors ran down groans and rumbles, as tons of sand shift slightly. One *Velociraptor* jumps onto the tail of the *Protoceratops*, ready to deliver the killer blow to her softer stomach. Both these raptors are staying away from the first one, neither wanting to get into similar trouble. They may have hunted together but they were not truly hunting cooperatively.

The top of the sand dune is unstable. The strong wind and effects of the three predators running down it causes a desert version of an avalanche. A massive section slips and tons of sand begin to slide toward the fighting animals.

The *Protoceratops* is still biting the first *Velociraptor.* Both animals are weak with pain but still alive. The *Velociraptor* manages to slip a daggerlike claw into her neck and she bites him even harder, clamping her jaws around him. At that moment, all four animals look up to see a wall of sand surging toward them.

The two other velociraptors hop off her body and run, easily escaping the sandy wall of death, leaving the two struggling animals to be buried. A wave of sand flows over and traps them.

There's so much sand that their chests are crushed and they cannot breathe. In less than a minute, both are dead. In this battle for life and death, both predator and prey are killed by their environment.

This fabulous fossil actually exists. We don't know if there was more than one Velociraptor and we have no idea if they fought at night or how the sand covered them but the fossil was found in Mongolia in 1971 and is now kept at the American Museum of Natural History. The fossil is known as the "Fighting Dinosaurs."

Fossil
Finder

This section gives you a beginner's guide on how to prepare fossils, once you've found them. There are lots of different ways to prepare fossils, and experts take years and years to learn the skills, but there are some quick and easy techniques you can use to start preparing fossils for yourself.

You can find all about what equipment you'll need to collect fossils and where to look for them in the other *So You Think You Know About . . . Dinosaurs?* books, but the most important rule is always to take an adult with you when you go fossil hunting and to ask an adult to help you when you are preparing any fossils you find.

Here are two easy ways you can start preparing fossils:

Physical preparation of ammonites

This first bit is usually best done on the beach where you find the fossils, so take a hammer, chisel and safety glasses with you. There's no point in taking lots and lots of rocks home with only one or two fossils. You'll have a bad back from lifting useless rocks.

Often, ammonites are preserved in limestone and can be found in what we call limestone "nodules." These nodules look like big round blobs of rock and can be found mixed in with other rock or lying on the beach. When you see one, you'll recognize it right away. It helps to have a good look at the nodule to see if there are any signs that a fossil might be inside before you start whacking it with a hammer.

When you have your nodule, look for any signs of weakness, such as a crack in the rock. If you see a crack, gently tap it with a geological hammer (or any small hammer will do).

Don't just hit it as hard as you can. If you do this, you'll probably injure yourself and damage the fossil. If it doesn't open after a few gentle taps, place the chisel along the crack and tap that instead. Once the nodule has split open, you will probably be left with the actual fossil on one half and the imprint (or the "trace fossil") on the other half. Usually, the ammonite will be beautifully exposed but if it needs to be cleaned any further, use a brush and a cocktail stick to clear away any tiny bits of rock left over. This can be done when you're at home. This should be enough to provide you with a cool fossil for your collection. Any more complicated than that and you will need some high-tech equipment.

Acid preparation of microfossils

Lumps of natural chalk can often be found on beaches. This white crumbly type of sedimentary rock is made up from ancient shells, crushed together.

Acid can be used to prepare small fossils like these. Although it can take a long time, it's a very good way to remove these tiny fossils, called microfossils. This method also means less risk to the fossils. Many paleontologists use a special chemical called acetic acid to dissolve the chalk. You may never have heard of this acid but you might have eaten it . . . it's the proper name for vinegar.

Place the chalk in a container with a diluted mixture of vinegar and water. To start with, use a ratio of 1:10, which means you need ten times more water than vinegar. Leave it to soak for between 1-3 days.

Use a fine mesh strainer and pour the acid solution away, trapping the "sludge" in the strainer. Then soak the sludge in water for a day, to stop the effects of the acid.

Strain it again and pour the sludge onto a tray. Either let it dry naturally for a day or two, or heat it in the oven for around an hour at 150° F. Don't strain it over a sink – you'll probably block it, and you won't be very popular at home!

If you are lucky enough to own a light microscope, that's great but if not, ask your teacher whether you can take the dried white powder to school. Keep it safe in a jar or envelope and take a little bit out to look at under the microscope. Get your teacher to show you how to do this.

Put a thin layer of the white powder on a microscope slide and have a look. There should be hundreds if not thousands of tiny fossils. There will be lots of different types of fossils too. For example, your sample should have lots of "forams" (short for foraminifera), which are single-celled organisms, with a little shell and ostracods (or "seed shrimps"), which are tiny relatives of crabs and shrimps.

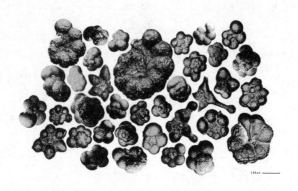

If you want to prepare your fossils using acid like this, then vinegar is great to use. Make sure you don't get it in your eyes and try to use white vinegar where you can, as it won't stain the fossils a funny color.

Quiz Answers

Page 42

Which phylum does the chimpanzee belong to?
Chordata.

What does *Homo sapiens* mean?
Thinking man.

**Which part of an animal's name comes first –
genus or species?**
Genus.

What group does *Velociraptor* belong to?
Dromaeosaurinae.

**When did velociraptors first appear and how long
did they survive?**
Mid Jurassic, surviving for more than 100 million years
until end of Cretaceous.

Name one of the best sites for finding feathered dinosaurs.
Liaoning in China.

Page 70

Which desert have *Velociraptor* fossils been found in?

Gobi Desert.

How many teeth did a *Velociraptor* have?

26–28.

What did *Velociraptor* use its 2.5-in. claws for?

Stabbing prey, delivering the killing blow.

What does endothermic mean?

Warm-blooded.

How much did a *Velociraptor* weigh?

28-40 lb.

How many fingers did *Velociraptor* have?

Three.

How many did you get?

Glossary

Adaptation This can be something physical or a
behavior that makes a species that little bit better
suited to its environment. It might be something like
hummingbirds having very light skeletons to make it
easier to fly, or a polar bear having a good sense of
smell to find food.

Carnivore An animal that survives by eating other
animals. Animals like lions, sharks and eagles are all
carnivores.

Concave If a shape has a curve that dips inward in
the middle, then it is concave. I always remember
it because it makes a little cave.

Convex If a shape has a curve that bulges outward
in the middle, then it is convex.

Endothermic This is the proper term for when we are
talking about being "warm-blooded." This means
that an animal makes and keeps its own body
temperature steady. Humans, whales and birds are
all endothermic.

Herbivore An animal that survives by eating plants. Animals like mice, pigeons and zebras are all herbivores.

Metabolism Your metabolism is all the stuff that goes on in your body (like chemical reactions) which your body needs to create energy in order to survive.

Oases Places in deserts that are green and lush. They are usually found where there is a stream or spring.

Retractable Something that can be extended and also pulled back and locked into place, like a cat's claws.

Talon A curved claw, mainly belonging to a bird of prey or a "raptor" dinosaur.

Theropod One of the many dinosaurs that have two legs and are usually carnivorous. *Tyrannosaurus rex, Allosaurus, Spinosaurus* and *Velociraptor* are all theropods.

Zygodactyly (*zy-go dac-til-ee*) A bird's foot on which two toes face forward and two face backward.

PICTURE CREDITS

Adobestock: 1, 12, 13, 16, 17, 18, 19, 20, 21, 22, 23, 34, 35, 36, 37, 47, 73, 76, 77, 89, 100, 110, 111. Depositphotos: 1, 17, 18, 19, 24, 30, 34, 35, 47, 81, 83, 88, 91, 96, 97, 99, 100. Ethan Kocak: 5, 6, 9, 11, 15, 22, 23, 24, 28, 29, 42, 43, 45, 46, 48, 49, 50, 51, 52, 53, 54, 55, 62, 63, 65, 70, 71, 73, 79, 85, 87, 92, 93, 94, 95, 98, 101, 103, 105, 109. E. Willoughby (commons-wikimedia. org): 33, 38, 64, 74. Fred Wierum (commons-wikimedia.org): 33, 39, 40, 41, 74. Gabriel Ugueto: 66-7. Scott Hartman: 25, 56-7, 60-1, 62-3. Thedinorocker@DeviantArt: 111.

Visit

www.bengarrod.co.uk

for lots more about
dinosaurs.

MEET DR. BEN GARROD

Dr. Ben Garrod is an evolutionary biologist, which means he studies how different animals change over time. He has worked worldwide with chimpanzees, whales, sharks and dinosaurs.

As a child growing up by the sea he fell in love with nature. He found his first fossil when he was very small and has loved dinosaurs ever since.

Ben is a TV presenter and a Teaching Fellow at Anglia Ruskin University in the UK.

bengarrod.co.uk

So You Think You Know About...
DINOSAURS?

HAVE YOU GOT THEM ALL?